Dedicated to Walter. Thank you for being my best friend. —Gideon

Dedicated to my sons, Max, Oliver, Gideon, and Nigel. Every day you teach me something new. I'm so proud to be your mom. —Rachel

PET THAT DOG!

A HANDBOOK FOR MAKING FOUR-LEGGED FRIENDS

by GIDEON KIDD & RACHEL BRAUNIGAN

of *I've Pet That Dog*

QUIRK BOOKS
PHILADELPHIA

Library of Congress Cataloging in Publication Data
Kidd, Gideon, author.
Pet that dog! : a handbook for making four-legged friends / by Gideon Kidd & Rachel Braunigan of I've Pet That Dog.
Summary: "A handbook that teaches kids how to meet, identify, and celebrate dogs" —Provided by publisher.
2020014707
LCSH: Dogs—Juvenile literature.
LCC SF427 .K389 2020 | DDC 636.7—dc23

ISBN: 978-1-68369-229-4

Printed in China

Typeset in Staring Contest, Ugiftig, Klinic Slab, and Iskra
Designed by Elissa Flanigan
Illustrations by Susann Hoffmann
Production management by John J. McGurk

Quirk Books
215 Church Street
Philadelphia, PA 19106
quirkbooks.com

10 9 8 7 6 5 4 3 2 1

Contents

Introduction
I've Pet That Dog!

My name is Gideon, and I love dogs! When I was 8 years old, I decided to keep track of every dog I met. I asked my mom if I could take a picture with each dog I petted so I could show everyone. Then I started the website IvePetThatDog.com, and I posted a picture of myself with each dog I've met. When I joined Twitter, I decided to share the dogs' stories along with the pictures.

So far, I have petted more than 1,000 different dogs, and each dog I meet teaches me something new. Some are playful. Some are fearful. Some are big, while some are tiny. Some dogs have jobs. Some dogs have homes and families, and some dogs are looking for a home. Each dog is different, and each dog has a their own story.

A dog is the best friend you will ever have, and they help you live your life to the fullest. They want to go where you go, play what you play, and eat what you eat. They will love you unconditionally and will always be happy to see you.

I have learned a lot about dogs over the years, and I hope this book helps you learn about them, too. There are so many dogs waiting to meet you!

How to Pet That Dog!

If you take the time to get to know a dog, you may make a new friend. But first, you have to know how to pet a dog.

It can be tempting to reach out and pet a cute dog as soon as you see one, but for your safety and the dog's, you should wait and be respectful of an animal's personal space—just like you do with people. Here are three important steps I follow before trying to make a new dog friend.

1. Ask the Caregiver.

Some dogs are afraid of strangers, protective of their family, or still learning good manners, so you should always ask for permission before petting a dog. It's easy to do. I always ask their caregiver, "Can I please pet your dog?" The caregiver knows their dog best, and they will tell you if you can pet their dog.

If the caregiver says no, that's okay! You can be a good friend to the dog by respecting this answer, saying thank you, and walking away.

Tips from Gideon

All dogs need to be socialized, some more than others. Meeting new people, meeting new dogs, and visiting new places all help dogs become more social.

2. Ask the Dog, Too.

Once you have permission from a dog's caregiver, you also need to ask the dog in a way that dogs understand.

A dog's most powerful sense is smell; they use their nose even more than their eyes or ears. Dogs sniff things to learn more about them, so you should give a dog the opportunity to smell you. The picture below shows you how. First, slowly reach out your hand, palm side up, toward the dog. This will give the dog a chance to get to know you.

A dog's body language will tell you if you can pet him. Body language is how a dog moves or responds. If he comes closer to you, leans into you, wags his tail happily, or rolls over, he feels comfortable with you. You can pet him!

If you reach out your hand and the dog backs away, barks, hides behind his caregiver, or growls, he is saying he does not want to be petted. That's okay! Sometimes a dog just needs to be left alone. (For more about dogs' body language, see page 16.)

3. Pet That Dog!

After getting a dog's permission, most people try to pet the top of a dog's head. But a dog that is meeting you for the first time might not like being touched there—or on his ears, face, or tail. Instead, it's better to pet the dog on the neck, shoulders, or side.

As you get to know a dog, you'll learn more about where they like to be petted. Some dogs love belly rubs, and some want strokes under their chin. I even met a dog who liked having his armpits scratched!

DOs and DON'Ts
for meeting dogs

DO ask the caregiver before petting a dog!

DO approach the dog from the front!

DO reach your hand out slowly in greeting.

DO be gentle and kind!

DO tell the dog she is a good dog!

DO be polite and say thank you to the caregiver!

DO record your meeting in your Dog Tracker on page 88!

DON'T reach out to a dog with sudden movements!

DON'T pull a dog's tail or fur!

DON'T hit or yell at a dog!

DON'T try to take away food or toys from a dog you don't know!

DON'T put your face right by a dog's face!

DON'T approach a dog from behind!

DON'T bend over a dog!

Now you know how to safely meet a dog! But a dog's body language expresses a lot more about what they are thinking or feeling. Read on to find out what else a dog may be telling you.

Meet Stella, the "Talking" Dog!

Stella is a dog who is learning to communicate using more than her body language and gestures. Stella is a Catahoula Leopard Dog and Blue Heeler mix whose caregiver, Christina Hunger, is a speech-language pathologist. Stella's caregiver made her a communication device consisting of a flat board with large buttons on it. When Stella pushes a button with her paw, it plays a recorded word. Stella walks onto the board and pushes buttons that say words like "eat," "play," "ball," or "outside." Stella has been taught to push buttons to ask for what she wants, express her feelings, and give directions. Stella often pushes two or three buttons in a row to say what she wants. For example, she may press "come," "eat," and "outside" to say she wants to eat first, then go outside. It is amazing that dogs are learning to communicate with people in our language! To follow along on Stella's language journey and learn more about her caregiver, follow @hunger4words on Instagram.

What's That Dog Telling You?

Have you ever seen a dog crouch or jump in a funny way? Or tuck his tail or wag like crazy? Just like people, dogs are always trying to tell us things. Learning these signals can help you communicate better with any dog you meet.

Match the descriptions below with the pictures that appear on pages 18 and 19 to better understand what your dog is communicating through their gestures and expressions.

When a dog is RELAXED AND HAPPY, he might look at you with his mouth open and his tongue hanging out.

When a dog WANTS TO PLAY, her body is loose and wiggly. She might lower the front of her body into a position called a "play bow," pick up a toy and toss it forward, or lunge headfirst under something or someone.

If a dog looks like he is frozen and not moving, it might be because he is UNSURE OR UNCOMFORTABLE.

Tips from Gideon

Many people think their dog is tired when she yawns, but she may actually be showing that she is nervous.

When a dog cowers, pants, or lowers their body to the ground with their ears back, they are **AFRAID**. They might also tuck their tails under their bodies.

When the fur on a dog's shoulders, spine or tail stands up it is called *hackles*. This means the dog is **UPSET, NERVOUS, OR EXCITED** about something. When you see hackles go up on a dog, back away to give him space so he can feel comfortable.

Fun Fact!

Dogs also use gestures and movements to communicate with humans. In 2018, researchers from the University of Salford in Manchester, England, published a study showing that dogs communicate most often to ask for food and drink, ask for the door to be opened, request a toy or bone, or ask for pets or scratches.

When a dog is hungry or thirsty, he may sit with one front paw held up.

When a dog wants to go outside, she may jump up or put both front paws onto something or someone.

If a dog wants petting or scratches, he might roll over, push his nose against you, or lick you!

Understanding Canine Body Language

Service Dogs

As you meet new dogs, you may see some dogs wearing vests that say *Service Dog*. These are not your average dogs. When these dogs have their vests on, it means that they are working.

There are many types of service and therapy dogs, including guide dogs, mobility assistance dogs, diabetic alert dogs, autism service dogs, medical alert dogs, hearing dogs, psychiatric service dogs, allergy detection dogs, and emotional support dogs. These working dogs help people navigate the world or alert them to a medical crisis. They provide comfort and support to people who have severe anxiety or post-traumatic stress disorder (PTSD). These dogs are heroes who help people and save lives every day.

I visited Retrieving Freedom, an organization that trains service dogs and places them with veterans and children with autism. It can take up to two years to train a service dog for this type of job. The dogs trained by Retrieving Freedom are taught extraordinary tasks, such as:

- Turning on and off lights
- Picking up or retrieving household objects
- Opening and closing doors
- Pushing panic buttons in case of an emergency
- Providing comfort when they sense anxiety

Service dogs and therapy dogs have very important jobs. **So, instead of petting a service dog, you should only admire them from a distance.** If these dogs are distracted from their work, they may not be able to do their job well.

To learn more about service dogs and Retrieving Freedom, I asked them some questions.

What type of dogs make the best service dog?

Service dogs have an exceptionally strong bond with their humans. A service dog must be accepting and social; no guarding or aggressive behavior is allowed. Because they accompany their humans in all public places, they need to be happy and friendly with the general public.

Labrador Retrievers, Golden Retrievers, Labradoodles and Goldendoodles are the most commonly used breeds, because they are natural retrievers.

How long does it take to train a service dog?

Training starts when puppies are seven to eight weeks old. We start with basic obedience and house training. Then puppies begin to go into public spaces and are exposed to a variety of places. The training continues until the dog is approximately 12 months of age. At that time the puppies come into the training center for formal training. The dogs begin learning the specific tasks that their humans will need. The dogs are placed in their homes at about two years of age. Follow-up training is continued throughout the dog's life.

What are some tasks that service dogs do for their jobs?

Autism Dogs are trained to help families with children on the Autism spectrum. The dogs perform many tasks, but the main task that dogs perform in public is "tethering." The child wears a waist leash that attaches to the dog's harness. If the child bolts or runs away, the dog is taught to lie down and prevent the child from getting very far away. One of the tasks that the dogs perform in the home is called "deep pressure." Many children on the Autism spectrum respond well to the feeling of deep pressure. The dog is taught to lie across the child's body to provide the pressure. The dogs can also go to the child and provide support if they are feeling anxiety and need a calming influence.

Service Dogs for veterans are taught to pick up items that are dropped, provide nightmare interruption, and position their bodies between the veteran and other people or objects if necessary. They also help with anxiety.

Where's That Dog?

Now that you know more about communicating with dogs, it's time to meet some four-legged friends!

Did you know that experts estimate there are nine hundred million dogs in the world? Before you set out to meet all of them, look close to home. The easiest place is right in your own town or city. There are probably many dogs right on your block or in your neighborhood. Getting to know the dogs who live around you is also a fun way to get to know your neighbors and community. See how many nearby places you can find a dog!

Another fun way to meet dogs is at local dog-friendly events. These types of events include Howl-o-ween pet parades, pet pictures at holiday times, dog festivals, and dog competitions. By doing some research online, in your local paper, or on social media, you can find out about dog-friendly events near you.

Now, turn the page to explore a map of common close-by places to find dogs to pet!

Meet That Dog!

(DOG)
PARK

OUTDOOR
COFFEE SHOP

FRESH

FARMER'S MARKET

LAKE

ANIMAL
SHELTER

WALKING to SCHOOL

VETERINERIAN'S
OFFICE *

*YOU CAN OFTEN FIND DOGS HERE,
BUT THEY MAY NOT WANT TO BE
PETTED. MANY DOGS GET NERVOUS WHEN
THEY HAVE TO SEE THE VET. WHEN YOU
SEE A DOG AT THE VET, IT'S BEST
TO LET THEM BE.

BIKE &
WALKING
TRAILS

PET SUPPLY STORES
& PET-FRIENDLY
STORES

Every Dog Has a Story

When you learn a dog's story,
you make a new friend.

I've met more than 1,000 dogs, and every dog I've met has a unique personality and their own story. My favorite part of petting dogs is learning about what makes them special. Here are some dogs I've met as well as stories about famous dogs from history that you will enjoy getting to know.

When I want to get to know a dog, I ask their caregivers questions. I've found that most people like to talk about their dogs and will be willing to answer your questions. Here are a few examples to get you started.

I ASK:

CAN I pet your dog?

WHAT is your dog's name?

WHAT kind of dog is she?

WHERE did you get your dog?

WHAT do you like most about your dog?

WHAT is unique about her?

WHAT does your dog like to do?

DOES she like to play with toys?

WHAT is her favorite food?

DO you have any funny stories about your dog?

WHAT was your dog's biggest adventure?

By asking these questions, I have heard many amazing stories! Turn the page to read about a few of my favorites.

I learned about REMUS. He was rescued from a home where he had never been

allowed outside. He'd never stepped on grass or gone for a walk. He was adopted by a different caregiver and now goes camping, canoeing, and hiking. He loves to be outside. He is still a little shy, but he has a dog best friend named Rory who is teaching him how to be a happy dog.

I learned about BAILEY. He is a 14-year-old Cockapoo who has had the same tennis ball his entire life. He refuses to

play with any other ball. He even refuses a different version of the same ball. Now Bailey's tennis ball is in two halves, but he still won't let it go.

I learned about PERSEPHONE. She got out of her yard one night during a snowstorm. Her caregiver had a sick child and a newborn baby at home, so he

couldn't go look for her. The next day he put up signs and called local shelters, but no one had seen her. Four years later, he received a call from a microchip company saying someone had found Persephone and was trying to claim the dog as their own. He had to file a police report to get Persephone home. Now Persephone is back with her family.

Tips from Gideon

Getting your dog **microchipped** can save her life. It doesn't cost much and is quick and easy to do! Microchips for pets are the size of a grain of rice. They are placed under the skin with a needle, like a shot. When a dog is found he can be scanned for a microchip to identify who his caregivers are and how to contact them. It's important that caregivers update their address and phone number with the microchip company if they move.

Amazing Dogs from History

Every dog changes the lives of the people who love them. But did you know that some dogs have changed the world? Let's meet some!

Barry
The Mountain Rescue Dog

Barry was a mountain rescue dog for the Great St. Bernard Hospice in the early 1800s. Located in the Alps, a mountain range in Europe, the Great St. Bernard Hospice was a monastery and a shelter for travelers, traders, and soldiers. The hospice was located along the Great St. Bernard Pass, a route through the mountains that connects Switzerland and Italy. The mountain pass was cold, dangerous, and one of the highest Alpine passes. It was the most important route across the Alps and was even used by the French military leader Napoleon Bonaparte and his troops.

Traveling along the pass was dangerous. People would get lost or injured and have no way to find shelter. Barry's

job was to help people find their way to the hospice, even in big snowstorms. He saved forty people!

Originally called mountain rescue dogs or hospice dogs, Barry and other dogs like him were bred at the hospice. Their breed was eventually named Saint Bernard, after the hospice. Barry and other mountain rescue dogs had such a good sense of smell that they could find people trapped under snow after an avalanche. These dogs would be assigned to go along with travelers on their route between the hospice and the Swiss town of Bourg-Saint-Pierre. The dogs could also find lost travelers and use their incredible sense of direction to get the travelers to shelter. The dogs used their bodies to keep the travelers warm. When

Napoleon and his army traveled along the pass between 1790 and 1810, every soldier survived. Many of the soldiers wrote that their survival was due to the dogs.

Barry retired when he was twelve years old and lived the rest of his life at the hospice. Today, the hospice is open as an inn. Saint Bernards no longer rescue people in the Alps, but they are still kept at the inn during the summer so tourists can see them. In winter, the dogs are housed at the Barry Foundation in Martingy, Switzerland, a village near the mountain pass. The Barry Foundation continues the tradition of breeding and raising Saint Bernards. In honor of the famous rescuer, one dog is always named Barry.

Togo
The Sled Dog Who Saved a Town

In 1995, the movie *Balto* was released. It told the story of the 1925 Serum Run, which was a journey to get life-saving medicine to the town of Nome, Alaska, by dog sled. The movie is named for one of the dogs who pulled the sled. Balto ran the final distance of the journey, bringing the medicine into Nome, and he was the one who was celebrated. However, it was another dog, named Togo, who ran the farthest and contributed the most to the mission. Togo was a twelve-year-old Siberian Husky and the lead sled dog who ran more than two hundred miles of the journey.

In the winter of 1924–1925, diphtheria was spreading through the town of Nome. Diphtheria is a bacterial infection that is often deadly. A medicine, known as a serum, was needed to stop the spread of the disease and save the people of the town.

The serum was transported by train for three hundred miles, but the winter weather made it impossible to get the serum closer to the town. There were no roads or railroads

between the towns. The harbor was frozen, so boats could not sail. Planes were unable to fly in the extreme cold because their open cockpits were exposed to the extreme temperatures. The serum was still almost 700 miles away, and many people were sick and could die if they did not receive it in time. A decision was made to use dog sled teams to bring the serum the rest of the way to Nome. At that time, dog sleds were used to deliver mail in Alaska, so this type of transportation seemed to be the only solution.

Togo was the lead sled dog for Leonhard Seppala, a dog breeder and racer. Togo led his team through brutally cold temperatures and dangerous snow and ice for a total of 261 miles. Balto was the lead sled dog for the final team, which carried the medicine for the final fifty-five miles into Nome. Because of Togo and Balto, the disease was stopped and the town was saved. Both dogs completed a heroic and dangerous run.

Fun Fact!

The oldest dog ever to live was Bluey. He was an Australian Cattle Dog who lived for twenty-nine years and five months!

Sergeant Stubby
World War I Hero

Sergeant Stubby was a Bull Terrier mix who served in the U.S. Army during World War I. He was the official mascot of the 102nd Infantry Regiment. Even though he was a dog, Stubby participated in seventeen battles. He is known as the most decorated war dog of World War I and was the only dog to be promoted to the rank of sergeant through combat.

Stubby was found as a stray by soldiers at Yale University in Hartford, Connecticut, where the 102nd Infantry trained. He was a brindle puppy with a short tail, so Corporal Robert Conroy named him Stubby. He was a very smart dog who learned the different training drills along with the soldiers. Stubby could even salute by bringing his paw up above his eye! He was so loved by the soldiers that Corporal Conroy snuck him over to France when the unit was deployed.

Stubby was very useful to the regiment. He could hear the sound of approaching bombs and smell gas attacks before the soldiers knew about them. It was reported that he once warned the sleeping soldiers of a gas attack by barking and biting them until they woke up. One night he even captured a German soldier by biting the man's pants and refusing to let go. Because he captured an enemy spy, he was given a promotion and achieved the rank of sergeant.

Stubby returned home safely from combat and was honored with parades. He was even able to meet President Woodrow Wilson. He lived the rest of his life with his caregiver, Corporal Conroy. When Conroy began studying law at Georgetown University, Stubby was made the mascot of the university. He went to football games and performed at halftime by pushing a football across the field.

The 2018 animated film *Sgt. Stubby: An American Hero* was based on Stubby's life and his adventures.

Bobbie the Wonder Dog
The Dog Who Traveled 2,500 Miles

Bobbie was a Scotch Collie and English Shepherd mix who lived in Silverton, Oregon. In August 1923, Bobbie and his family went on a car trip to Wolcott, Indiana. Each night during the trip, the family stopped and slept at a service station. When they reached Wolcott, Bobbie was attacked by three dogs and ran away. His family desperately tried to find him but could not. They finally had to return home to Oregon without Bobbie.

Six months later, in February 1924, Bobbie showed up back home in Silverton, Oregon. He was very skinny and dirty. Bobbie traveled at least 2,500 miles to get back to his family.

Bobbie's story was told in the newspaper and even in "Ripley's Believe It or Not," a newspaper column printed throughout the country. As his story spread, people began

to contact his family and say that they had seen Bobbie or taken care of him along the way. His family discovered that Bobbie had returned to every service station where they had spent the night on their way to Indiana.

Each year, Silverton, Oregon, has a pet parade that honors the memory of Bobbie the Wonder Dog. The first parade was held in 1932, and the Grand Marshall was Bobbie's son, Pal. It is the longest running pet parade in the United States. Children, adults, and pets can all march in the parade. You don't even have to register—just show up in Silverton on the third Saturday in May!

Buddy
The First Seeing Eye Dog in the United States

Morris Frank was born in 1908. As a child, he lost an eye when he was riding on a horse and ran into a tree. When he was 16 years old, he lost his other eye in a boxing match. He went to college at Vanderbilt University, paying a helper to guide him to and from classes. He disliked having a person with him at all times, especially when he went on dates.

In 1927, Frank read an article about German dogs who were trained to help blind war veterans. This article was written by a dog breeder living in Switzerland named Dorothy Harrison Eustis. Frank went to Switzerland to meet with the breeder and learn more about these dogs.

During his visit, Frank met a female German Shepherd named Kiss. He decided to change her name to Buddy because he didn't want to call out- "Kiss!" when he wanted her attention.

In 1928, Frank and Buddy returned to the United States and were swarmed with reporters wanting to learn about Buddy. Frank had Buddy guide him across a busy city street while the reporters watched. This demonstration of Buddy's abilities led to newspaper articles and excitement all over the country. Frank reported that Buddy allowed him to do things he had not been able to do on his own. He also said that people now approached him without fear, instead of avoiding him. He credited Buddy with changing his life.

In 1929, Morris Frank and Dorothy Harrison Eustis founded the Seeing Eye, the first modern guide dog school and the first guide dog school in the United States. As of this writing, the Seeing Eye has trained more than 17,000 guide dogs.

Smoky
The First Known Therapy Dog

While stationed in New Guinea, a large island north of Australia, in March 1944, an American soldier found a small Yorkshire Terrier whimpering in the brush. He gave the dog to Bill Wynne, a soldier in his unit who liked dogs. Wynne named the Yorkie Smoky. She was a tiny dog, said to stand only as tall as the top of his boots. She was named for her smoky blue-gray fur. Wynne began training Smoky to do tricks, such as sit and heel. He even taught her to play dead when he said "Bang."

Wynne entered Smoky in a contest run by the military magazine *Yank* to find the best military mascot. He placed Smoky in his helmet and took a picture of her. He also created a small parachute and captured pictures of her wearing it and floating to the ground.

Wynne became sick with dengue fever. Smoky was brought to visit him in the hospital, and the staff brought Smoky around to visit the other soldiers. The soldiers cheered up and enjoyed seeing and petting Smoky. She took to regularly visiting the patients in the hospital until Wynne recovered.

Besides keeping up morale and comforting the soldiers, Smoky assisted the soldiers in their mission. She once helped to restore communications by crawling through a small and dangerous underground tunnel with wires attached to her collar. Smoky emerged from the tunnel unhurt, and the soldiers were able to reattach the wires without any loss of life. Smoky also went along on twelve aerial combat missions, survived a kamikaze attack, and endured a typhoon during her time with the troops. For her service, she was awarded eight battle stars.

When it was time for Bill Wynne to return to the United States., he hid Smoky in an oxygen mask in order to smuggle her home with him. Once back home, they continued to visit hospitalized veterans and injured soldiers until Smoky's death in 1957. Because of her work comforting soldiers, Smoky is considered the first therapy dog.

After Smoky's death, Wynne learned that a field nurse had lost a female Yorkshire Terrier named Christmas while stationed in New Guinea in 1944. Because Yorkies were not normally found in New Guinea at this time, it appeared that Christmas and Smoky were the same dog. The only mystery that remained was how Smoky was found 180 miles away at a completely different base. Wynne believed that Smoky, aka Christmas, accidently hitched a ride with the comedian Bob Hope, who traveled from base to base entertaining U.S. military troops.

Fun Fact!

Small dogs aim higher when they pee. Researchers don't know why they do this, but one theory is that they are trying to appear larger than they are and to avoid fights with other dogs.

Bosco
The First Dog Mayor

Bosco was a Labrador mix who was the very first dog mayor. He served as mayor of Sunol, California, from 1981 until 1994, when he died. Bosco's candidacy started out as a joke, but he quickly became the most popular candidate in the race. He ran as a "Re-Pup-Lican" and his campaign slogan was, "A bone in every dish, a cat in every tree, and a fire hydrant on every corner." He beat his HUMAN opponents by a landslide!

Bosco's duties as mayor were only ceremonial. He represented the town at events, led the annual Halloween parade, and often appeared in a tuxedo. However, he was the focus of a real international controversy in 1989 when the Chinese communist newspaper *People's Daily* published an article claiming that Bosco's election was proof that democratic voting doesn't work. As a result, Bosco was a featured guest at a pro-democracy rally.

Sunol had a population of about 1,000 people, and everyone knew Bosco. The four-legged mayor liked to wander the town, stopping in local taverns for food and attention. He would growl if someone didn't share their food! He especially loved beef jerky.

Bosco ran free around the whole town. More than once, Bosco disappeared for a few days. One time, he was found stuck in someone's garage. Another time, he fell asleep in the back of a pick-up truck and wound up in Oregon.

In 2008, a life-size bronze statue of Bosco was installed outside the Sunol post office. If you visit the town, you can stop and pet Bosco for good luck. A local bar and grill is named after the former mayor. It is called Bosco's Bones and Brew. The bar has a stuffed dog with a keg of beer inside it. If you ask the bartender for a pint of Bosco's brew, the leg of the stuffed dog is lifted and beer comes out as if the dog is peeing!

More Amazing Dogs from History

The first canine movie star was **BLAIR**, a collie who starred in the 1905 silent film *Rescued by Rover*. The movie was a hit, and "Rover" went on to become one of the most popular dog names.

The old saying "fighting like cats and dogs" doesn't apply to **GINNY**, a schnauzer/Siberian husky mix who had a knack for helping cats in need. She was named Cat of the Year in 1998 by the Westchester Cat Show, in appreciation for her many kitty rescues.

A bulldog named **HANDSOME DAN** became the first live college mascot back in 1889, when Yale University announced that he would represent the school. He held the job until his death in 1898. Since then, there have been 17 other "Handsome Dans," including a female named Bingo.

RICO, a clever border collie from Germany, made the news back in 2004. Rico could understand 200 simple words and was able to identify and fetch dozens of toys.

The expedition of Meriwether Lewis and William Clark in the 1800s had an important member: a fearless black Newfoundland named **SEAMAN**. The dog's barking warned the explorers of dangers and his hunting skills helped keep them alive in the wilderness.

How to Care for a Dog

Now that you know more
about dogs, it's time to learn
how to take care of one!

Adding a dog to your family is such an exciting, joyful step! Whether you already have a dog, you're dreaming of getting one, or you just like playing with dogs, it's important to know how to care for a new canine companion.

Adopting a Dog

When you decide you're ready to adopt a dog, you also need to figure out where to find one. Fortunately, there are many places to find all types of dogs.

Millions of dogs are currently without a home. One simple way to help is to adopt a dog at your local shelter or rescue organization. If you adopt a dog, you are not only giving a needy animal a home but also making room in a shelter or at a rescue organization so that they can help another dog.

Your local shelter will be able to help you find the perfect dog for your home. Whether you want a dog who is small, large, filled with energy, cuddly, playful, older, or young, the shelter staff can introduce you to a dog who is right for you and your family.

Adopting a dog often costs a lot less than buying a dog from a breeder. Your adoption cost helps support the shelter and pays for the cost to neuter or spay your pup. Spaying/neutering means that your dog will not be able to have puppies. This is important because there are already so many dogs who need homes. It can also help reduce the chances of some forms of illness in your pet.

If you choose to adopt a dog, don't overlook the older dogs! These dogs are more likely to be house-trained and may even have more manners than a younger, wilder puppy. Older dogs can be a perfect fit for families or for someone who wants a companion.

An easy way to find all of the dogs available in your area is to look on the website of your local shelters or ASPCA branch, or visit Petfinder.com. On these sites, you can find pictures and information posted by shelters about the dogs they have available for adoption. You can even search for specific breeds, ages, or behavior types.

Tips from Gideon

If you want a specific breed of dog, but also want to adopt, there are ways to do it! Talk to your local shelter or rescue and let them know what kind of dog you are looking for. (Some states even have breed-specific rescues.) Make sure you fill out an application and are approved, so that when the dog you want becomes available, you can be first on the list! Lastly, don't ignore mixes. These shelter specials may not be purebred, but they are often awesome, loving dogs! A Pug mix can give you all the personality of their breed, and by adopting them, you save a dog who needs a home.

If you are unsure that you want a dog, or you can only commit to having one for a limited time, fostering may be for you. Many rescues place their dogs with foster families so the pups can adapt to living in a home and with a family. Foster placements can help a dog work through problems, like learning how to use a leash or going to the bathroom outside. Fostering performs an important job. It keeps the dogs out of shelters and cages while also teaching them how to behave so that they can successfully be adopted. Sometimes there is a foster fail. This sounds like a bad thing, but it is actually something very happy: It's when a family decides to stop fostering the dog and to adopt the pup instead!

If you decide you want a purebred dog, choosing a reputable breeder is important. A good breeder will know a lot about the dogs they breed. Their dogs will be in good health and housed in clean areas. They will provide you with documentation of medical screenings and vet appointments. They will expect you to visit and meet you before allowing you to take home a puppy. Good breeders love their dogs and want to make sure that your home is a good fit. Many reputable breeders even insist on having your family sign a contract to take good care of the dog. Do your research and ask the breeder for references. A good breeder will be able to give you the names of caregivers who are raising their dogs, as well as veterinarians who have provided them with care.

A Dog's Basic Needs

My family adopted Cookie, a three-year-old Beagle–Hound mix. He was found as a stray and brought to the animal shelter to find a home. Cookie is loving and playful, but he is often nervous and afraid. He loves to play with his toys and snuggle with me on the couch. My family is helping Cookie learn to walk on a leash and to feel comfortable in our home. Cookie is helping us learn what he needs to feel safe and happy.

A healthy and happy dog needs much more than food and love. Dogs need our time, energy, veterinary care, and training. When you adopt a dog, you're promising to give that dog a forever home. And remember: if you adopt a puppy, just like human babies, they grow up! Make sure you want that cute puppy and the equally adorable grown-up dog she will become!

Dogs need a safe, loving home. It helps if they can have their own special place to sleep. Your dog may wind up sleeping in your bed, or on the couch, or even on the floor, but a dog bed or crate of his own will help him feel like he belongs. (See page 61 for more on crate training.) Some dogs even like to snuggle with a blanket or a piece of clothing that smells like their caregiver.

Dogs need exercise to live a healthy life. Getting their energy out also helps them behave; tired dogs are less likely to be destructive dogs!

Here are some ways
to keep your dog happy and active.

PLAY with your dog in the backyard

GO for walks with your dog in your neighborhood

BRING your dog to play with other dogs at the dog park

TAKE your dog jogging with you

MAKE a scavenger hunt with treats when you're stuck inside! Mental exercises like this are important for dogs, too.

Tips from Gideon

Some dogs like to swim. If you live near a lake, take your dog to play there. Don't forget to make sure the lake is clean! Some forms of algae can be dangerous for dogs.

Just like humans, dogs need healthy food to eat. Your vet can help you choose which food is right for your dog. Also, make sure your dog always has clean, fresh water in their bowl. Change it daily!

Dogs also need grooming. How much grooming your dog needs depends on the type of dog she is. Some breeds only need baths and brushing, but others have hair that grows very long and needs to be trimmed, just like people's hair does. Many people can give their dogs baths, but not everyone can groom their own dogs or trim their nails. You might need to bring your dog to a professional groomer to help her stay comfortable and look her best.

Don't forget about toys! Many dogs like to chew, and it's better for them to chew on a toy shoe than on your real shoe. Squeaky toys, stuffed animals, rope pulls, and balls can give your dog something to do and can also be a way for you to play with your dog. There are even puzzle toys, which are both fun *and* provide your dog with mental stimulation.

Fun Fact!

The two main reasons that dogs dig are to expose cooler dirt when they are hot and to hide a favorite toy or treat.

Training and Manners

An important part of caring for a dog is training. While you may not need your dog to perform tricks, it is important for him to know how to go to the bathroom outside, come when called, sit, and walk on a leash. These basic commands help a dog live successfully with people. They also help your dog understand the rules and what is expected of him. Expecting your dog to sit on command but never teaching him this skill will be confusing for him. If your dog knows how to follow your commands early on, he will be safer, happier, and better behaved.

The first thing dogs must learn is to go to the bathroom outside. Teaching him this skill can take a lot of time and patience! He should be brought outside first thing in the morning, after eating or drinking, right after he wakes up from a nap, after playing, and at night before bed. If you bring him outside on a leash to the same area each time, he will begin to associate both the leash and the area outside with going to the bathroom.

Each time your pup goes to the bathroom outside, celebrate! Give him a treat, a ton of pets, and lots of praise. Just like people, dogs learn best through positive reinforcement, instead of anger. Rewarding your pup for doing the right things encourages him to keep doing the right thing.

If your dog has an accident, never yell, get mad, or hit her. Instead, just clean it up and make sure to get rid of any odors. With a schedule, patience, and love, your dog will learn to go to the bathroom outside.

Fun Fact!

Dogs poop in alignment with the north-south axis of the Earth's magnetic field. It is not known why.

A dog needs to adjust to wearing a collar or harness and a leash. Putting these on each time you take your dog outside to go to the bathroom can help him get comfortable. Harnesses often work best because they don't hurt your dog, but they do help control him and stop him from lunging at exciting things like squirrels or other dogs. Whether you use a collar or a harness, soft materials like nylon or padded mesh are best.

It takes time and practice for your dog to learn to walk on a leash. Short sessions are best until your dog is more comfortable wearing the leash. Never drag your dog or pull him harshly. Reward him with bite-size training treats for staying near you and walking without pulling.

Training works best when you practice for just a few minutes at a time and there are no distractions. Teaching your dog to come when called and to sit are the most important commands. These commands may be needed in an emergency situation. By keeping the training fun and positive, your dog will want to work with you. Just like housetraining, when your dog performs the commands correctly, celebrate! Give him praise, pets, and a treat. The more your dog enjoys following directions, the more obedient he will be.

Crate Training

Some dogs and puppies do best with crate training. If your dog is chewing the furniture or going to the bathroom where he shouldn't, crate training gives him a safe, calm spot to rest when you can't supervise him. As long as they are not left too long, most dogs will not go to the bathroom in the same place where they sleep. Crates can be like a cozy den, and many dogs enjoy having their own quiet spot.

Crates should be a happy place for your dog. Make sure she has had time to play and exercise before putting her in her crate. Give her treats and special chew toys when she is there. Allow her to sleep with a favorite blanket. Always remove your dog's harness or collar before she goes in the crate. This keeps your dog safe and ensures the collar will not become snagged or caught on any part of the crate. All of these things make the crate a calm, restful place instead of a place where she doesn't want to be.

It is important to use time in the crate as a way to rest, instead of a punishment. Dogs need exercise, attention, and love. If they spend too much time confined, they will become unhappy and may develop behavior problems.

Keep in mind that crate training is not for all dogs. Some dogs have spent a long time in shelters or in small spaces, and they fear crates. You know your dog best! If crate training doesn't work for you or your dog, that's okay!

What If I'm Allergic to Dogs?

Many people love dogs but are also allergic to them. If you sneeze, get a runny nose, or have other reactions when around dogs, you are most likely allergic to a protein in a dog's saliva or urine. This protein sticks to a dog's skin and is shed as dander when they shed their fur.

Some dogs are known as *hypoallergenic*, which means they do not cause an allergic reaction. In reality, no dogs

are truly hypoallergenic. All dogs shed some dander and can cause an allergic reaction. But some dogs are less likely to cause problems for allergy sufferers. If you are allergic to dogs, you might still be able to have one of your own by choosing a breed that does not shed their hair or that sheds less than other dogs.

Dogs who don't shed very much typically have coats that need to be trimmed because they grow long. Some people refer to this kind of coat as hair, instead of fur. Some examples of dogs who shed the least are:

- Afghan Hounds
- American Hairless Terrier
- Bedlington Terrier
- Bichon Frise
- Chinese Crested
- Schnauzer
- Irish Water Spaniel
- Maltese
- Poodle
- Soft-Coated Wheaten Terrier
- Poodle mixes, like goldendoodles, labradoodles, cavapoos, whoodles, and more.

Low-shed dogs are often very popular and can be hard to find in your local shelter, so don't forget to check breed-specific rescue groups, which can pair you with a dog in need.

Every person and every dog is different. If you have allergies, spend some time around the dog you want to adopt before bringing him home. To reduce pet allergens, vacuum your home often, as well as brush and bathe your dog regularly.

Tips from Gideon

If you have allergies to pet dander or you just can't adopt a dog right now, you can still enjoy dogs' company. Local shelters and rescues almost always need volunteers. Your time and love can help make a difference in a dog's life. It will probably make a difference in your life, too!

If you would like to help dogs but can't commit to having a dog long-term, fostering might be for you. Ask your local rescue how you can help.

Ask the Expert!

To find out more about caring for dogs, I interviewed Dr. Chad Smith, a veterinarian at Taylor Veterinary Hospital in Cedar Falls, Iowa. In addition to dogs, he also treats cats, guinea pigs, and other household pets. Dr. Smith decided he wanted to be a veterinarian when he was eight years old.

What do you think is important for people to know before adopting a dog?

Before you adopt a dog, ask yourself:

- Am I willing to care for this dog for the next 10 to 15 years?
- What kind of dog fits my life? Do I want a dog to go running with me or one that likes to cuddle on the couch? Do I have enough space for a big dog, or is my space better suited to a small dog?
- Do I have time to walk the dog, play with the dog, brush the dog's teeth, et cetera?
- Do I have enough money to pay for the dog's food and supplies, grooming, boarding while I'm on vacation, vet bills, et cetera? What if there is an unexpected expense when the dog gets sick?

When do you need to take your dog to the vet?

I recommend taking your puppy or dog to a veterinarian within the first couple days after taking them home. Your vet will do a thorough exam to look for current or potential problems. The vet will also check for intestinal parasites, start heartworm/flea/tick prevention medicine, and go over the vaccinations your pet needs. Your vet will also talk to you about training your puppy or dog.

Do dogs get shots?

Just like people, it is very important that your dog be up-to-date on vaccinations to keep him or her healthy. Depending on where you live, and if your dog spends a lot of time outside or goes to grooming, daycare, or boarding, your veterinarian may recommend different vaccinations to help protect him or her. Regardless of where they live, all dogs should get the rabies and distemper-parvovirus combination vaccinations.

How do you know if your dog is sick?

Knowing how your dog acts normally is very important to determine if your pet is sick. Just like us, a sick pet will act more tired, not eat or drink as well, and could show signs like vomiting or diarrhea.

What kind of food should you feed your dog?

I recommend feeding a good-quality food and sticking with it. The more often you change the food, the more chances your dog will develop an upset stomach. A brand-name food company that employs a veterinary nutritionist is usually a safe place to start when choosing a food. Ask your veterinarian for their recommendations.

Are there some things a dog should never eat?

Dogs are known to eat just about anything . . .especially if it is left lying around. It is very important that your dog not eat chocolate (dark chocolate is worse for dogs than milk chocolate), grapes, raisins, macadamia nuts, garlic, or onions. In addition to those, any sugar-free food that contains xylitol (like some chewing gums) can be very dangerous for dogs.

What can you do if your dog is having problems, like chewing or peeing on the floor?

If your dog is showing any behavioral issues, he or she may be sick. I recommend taking your dog to the veterinarian for a complete evaluation. In addition to an exam, this could include getting a blood or urine sample, taking X-rays, or various other tests. If a medical problem is not found, your veterinarian will probably talk to you about how to retrain your dog or what you can do to help stop the problem.

What is your favorite thing about your dog?

I have a nine-year-old dog named Honey B. She is a black Lab–red heeler mix and very energetic! Dogs have many wonderful qualities, but my favorite thing about Honey B. is that her main goal in life, other than eating, is to get attention. She loves to see me when I come home and immediately rolls over to have her belly rubbed.

Name That Dog!

Now that you've learned all about dogs,
it's time to name your future pup.

If you had a dog, would you name her after a person, a food, or something else entirely? This quiz will give you ideas for all kinds of names!

When my family and I chose our dogs' names, we all worked together to find ones that suited each dog the best. We recently adopted a stray from our local shelter. My brother and I decided that Cookie was a good name for him because he is so sweet and everyone loves cookies! Sometimes it's just that simple.

Now let's try something fun—finding a silly dog name from the lists on the next pages. Follow the directions and see what you come up with. I should name my dog Walter Bouncy Floofenbutt!

For your dog's first name,
choose the date you were born:

1. Bartholomew
2. Charlie
3. Bailey
4. Pop Tart
5. Duke/Duchess
6. Daffodil
7. Potato
8. Freckles
9. Matilda
10. Waffle
11. Morris
12. Howard
13. Marmalade
14. Prince/Princess
15. Chester
16. Peanut
17. Apollo
18. Cupcake
19. Walter
20. Hank
21. Ruby
22. Tater Tot
23. Marshmallow
24. Lucky
25. Buttercup
26. Hazelnut
27. Coco
28. Oscar
29. Petunia
30. King/Queen
31. Otis

For your dog's middle name,
choose the first letter of your first name:

A or B: Monster	**O or P:** Sleepy
C or D: Fancy	**Q or R:** Chonky
E or F: Goofy	**S or T:** Sausage
G or H: Bouncy	**U or V:** Snuggly
I or J: Snorfle	**W or X:** Grumpy
K or L: Fuzzy	**Y or Z:** Drooly
M or N: Chewy	

And finally, for your dog's last name,
choose the first letter of your last name:

A or B: Pants	**O or P:** Waddler
C or D: Bottom	**Q or R:** Wigglehound
E or F: McDoggins	**S or T:** Snacker
G or H: Muffin	**U or V:** Paws
I or J: Scruffmaster	**W or X:** Barksalot
K or L: Floofenbutt	**Y or Z:** Waggington
M or N: Snackhound	

Personality Quiz

Have you ever wondered what
kind of dog you would be?

Just like humans, dogs have different personalities and behaviors. Take this quiz to find out what kind of dog you resemble most.

1. How much do you like to be around people?

A. I'm a little shy; lots of people make me nervous.

B. I enjoy being with people, but I also need some time alone.

C. I love people! Too much time alone and I get cranky.

D. I love being with my family. Wherever they go, I go.

E. I hate being alone. Please don't leave!

F. I like being around people as long as I have something to do.

2. Where would you like to live?

A. I would enjoy living in an apartment building in a big city.

B. I would do well in a city, as long as I could get out regularly and exercise in the park.

C. I can live anywhere as long as there's room to play!

D. I would love to live somewhere I can see birds and animals outside.

E. I would like a home with a yard. If it is near a lake, I am even happier!

F. I need a lot of space to spread out. A farm or a home with a large yard would make me happiest.

3. Which of these things would bother you the most?

A. My best friend wants to go somewhere without me.

B. I'm stuck inside all day.

C. I missed a meal.

D. Someone is telling me to do something I don't want to do.

E. No one is around to play with me.

F. I'm not able to help someone.

4. What is your favorite way to spend a weekend?

A. I like to snuggle under the blankets.

B. I love getting pampered at the spa.

C. I could spend all weekend lounging on the couch watching movies.

D. I enjoy walking in the woods.

E. Playing sports with my friends is the perfect way to spend the weekend.

F. I want to go swimming!

5. What is your best quality?

A. I am loyal.

B. I am protective of those I love.

C. I make everyone laugh.

D. I am determined.

E. I get along with everyone.

F. I work hard.

6. It's chilly outside! Would you like a sweater?

A. I'm not going out there!

B. I only want a sweater if it makes me look cute.

C. Who wouldn't want a cozy sweater?

D. As soon as I get moving around, I'll be good.

E. No, thanks!

F. I love the cold! I could stay out here for hours!!

7. What is your bad habit?

A. I can get jealous.

B. I talk all the time.

C. I can sleep the day away.

D. I can be stubborn.

E. I can be a little too energetic and rambunctious.

F. I hate to be bored.

8. What is your best feature?

A. My brain.

B. My hair.

C. My laugh.

D. My eyes.

E. My smile.

F. My ability to be noticed whenever I enter a room.

Score Your Answers!

A = 1 B = 2 C = 3 D = 4 E = 5 F = 6

After scoring each answer, add up the total and write that number in the space below.

TOTAL:

Now, turn the page, look for your number, and see what kind of dog you are!

8-14: You are a **Chihuahua!** You are very loyal to the people in your life. Your friends and family are everything to you. You like to be included in the fun and get sad if you are alone too much.

15-20: You are a **Pomeranian!** There is nothing shy about you. You prefer to look your best and enjoy being active. You love to talk and will share your opinions with everyone.

21-27: You are a **Pug!** You are the clown in your family. You make everyone laugh. Sleep and food are very important to you. You'll never turn down a tasty treat or a nap on the couch.

28–34: You are a **Basset Hound!** You can be stubborn, but your puppy-dog eyes make people give in to you. You love to be outdoors and watch wildlife. You are probably a pretty good singer. You can howl a sad song like no one else!

35–41: You are a **Labrador Retriever!** You have lots of energy and like to be active. You probably participate in sports and love being on a team with your friends. You get along with everyone and are easy to please.

42–48: You are a **Newfoundland!** You like to be useful and help people. You are calm and patient. You love to swim and play in the water. You may stand out in a crowd, but it's your kindness that is noticed most.

Dog Tracker

Use this section to write about
the dogs you meet, like I do!

I keep track of all the dogs I meet by taking a picture with them and writing about them. I like to see how many breeds I can meet and how many unique dogs I can find. Use this section to write about all the different dogs you meet.

Portuguese WATER DOG

BULLDOG

Cardigan WELSH CORGI

Airedale TERRIER

CHOW CHOW

Papillon

SENIOR Dog

GREATER SWISS Mountain Dog

PUPPY (Golden Retriever)

BULL TERRIER

SCHNAUZER

HAVANESE

Breeds

. . . .

☐ **Affenpinscher**

NAME: _____ DATE: _____

NOTES: _____

_____

☐ **Afghan Hound**

NAME: _____ DATE: _____

NOTES: _____

_____

☐ **Airedale Terrier**

NAME: _____ DATE: _____

NOTES: _____

_____

☐ **Akita**

NAME: _____ DATE: _____

NOTES: _____

_____

☐ **Alaskan Malamute**

NAME: _____ DATE: _____

NOTES: _____

_____

☐ **American English Coonhound**

NAME: _____ DATE: _____

NOTES: _____

_____

☐ **American Eskimo Dog**

NAME: _____ DATE: _____

NOTES: _____

_____

☐ **American Foxhound**

NAME: _____ DATE: _____

NOTES: _____

_____

☐ **American Hairless Terrier**

NAME: _____ DATE: _____

NOTES: _____

_____

☐ **American Shephard**

NAME: _____ DATE: _____

NOTES: _____

_____

☐ **American Staffordshire Terrier**

NAME: _____ DATE: _____

NOTES: _____

_____

☐ American Water Spaniel

NAME: _____ DATE: _____

NOTES: _____

_____

☐ Anatolian Shepherd Dog

NAME: _____ DATE: _____

NOTES: _____

_____

☐ Australian Cattle Dog

NAME: _____ DATE: _____

NOTES: _____

_____

☐ Australian Shepherd

NAME: _____ DATE: _____

NOTES: _____

_____

☐ Australian Terrier

NAME: _____ DATE: _____

NOTES: _____

_____

☐ Basenji

NAME: _____ DATE: _____

NOTES: _____

_____

☐ Basset Griffon Vendéen

NAME: _____ DATE: _____

NOTES: _____

_____

☐ Basset Hound

NAME: _____ DATE: _____

NOTES: _____

_____

☐ Beagle

NAME: _____ DATE: _____

NOTES: _____

_____

☐ Bearded Collie

NAME: _____ DATE: _____

NOTES: _____

_____

☐ Bedlington Terrier

NAME: _____ DATE: _____

NOTES: _____

_____

☐ Bernese Mountain Dog

NAME: _____ DATE: _____

NOTES: _____

_____

☐ **Bichon Frise**

NAME: _____ DATE: _____

NOTES: _____

_____

☐ **Bloodhound**

NAME: _____ DATE: _____

NOTES: _____

_____

☐ **Boerboel**

NAME: _____ DATE: _____

NOTES: _____

_____

☐ **Border Collie**

NAME: _____ DATE: _____

NOTES: _____

_____

☐ **Border Terrier**

NAME: _____ DATE: _____

NOTES: _____

_____

☐ **Borzoi**

NAME: _____ DATE: _____

NOTES: _____

_____

☐ Boston Terrier

NAME: _____ DATE: _____

NOTES: _____

_____

☐ Bouvier des Flandres

NAME: _____ DATE: _____

NOTES: _____

_____

☐ Boxer

NAME: _____ DATE: _____

NOTES: _____

_____

☐ Briard

NAME: _____ DATE: _____

NOTES: _____

_____

☐ Brittany Spaniel

NAME: _____ DATE: _____

NOTES: _____

_____

☐ Brussels Griffon

NAME: _____ DATE: _____

NOTES: _____

_____

☐ Bulldog

NAME: _____ DATE: _____

NOTES: _____

_____

☐ Bullmastiff

NAME: _____ DATE: _____

NOTES: _____

_____

☐ Bull Terrier

NAME: _____ DATE: _____

NOTES: _____

_____

☐ Cairn Terrier

NAME: _____ DATE: _____

NOTES: _____

_____

☐ Canaan Dog

NAME: _____ DATE: _____

NOTES: _____

_____

☐ Cane Corso

NAME: _____ DATE: _____

NOTES: _____

_____

☐ Cardigan Welsh Corgi

NAME: _____ DATE: _____

NOTES: _____

_____

☐ Cavalier King Charles Spaniel

NAME: _____ DATE: _____

NOTES: _____

_____

☐ Cesky Terrier

NAME: _____ DATE: _____

NOTES: _____

_____

☐ Chesapeake Bay Retriever

NAME: _____ DATE: _____

NOTES: _____

_____

☐ Chihuahua

NAME: _____ DATE: _____

NOTES: _____

_____

☐ Chinese Crested

NAME: _____ DATE: _____

NOTES: _____

_____

☐ Chinese Shar-Pei

NAME: _____ DATE: _____

NOTES: _____

_____

☐ Chinook

NAME: _____ DATE: _____

NOTES: _____

_____

☐ Chow Chow

NAME: _____ DATE: _____

NOTES: _____

_____

☐ Cirneco dell'Etna

NAME: _____ DATE: _____

NOTES: _____

_____

☐ Clumber Spaniel

NAME: _____ DATE: _____

NOTES: _____

_____

☐ Cocker Spaniel

NAME: _____ DATE: _____

NOTES: _____

_____

☐ **Collie**

NAME: _____ DATE: _____

NOTES: _____

_____

☐ **Coonhound**

NAME: _____ DATE: _____

NOTES: _____

_____

☐ **Curly-Coated Retriever**

NAME: _____ DATE: _____

NOTES: _____

_____

☐ **Dachshund**

NAME: _____ DATE: _____

NOTES: _____

_____

☐ **Dalmatian**

NAME: _____ DATE: _____

NOTES: _____

_____

☐ **Dandie Dinmont Terrier**

NAME: _____ DATE: _____

NOTES: _____

_____

☐ Doberman Pinscher

NAME: _____ DATE: _____

NOTES: _____

_____

☐ English Cocker Spaniel

NAME: _____ DATE: _____

NOTES: _____

_____

☐ English Foxhound

NAME: _____ DATE: _____

NOTES: _____

_____

☐ English Setter

NAME: _____ DATE: _____

NOTES: _____

_____

☐ English Springer Spaniel

NAME: _____ DATE: _____

NOTES: _____

_____

☐ English Toy Spaniel

NAME: _____ DATE: _____

NOTES: _____

_____

☐ **Finnish Lapphund**

NAME: _____ DATE: _____

NOTES: _____

_____

☐ **Flat-Coated Retriever**

NAME: _____ DATE: _____

NOTES: _____

_____

☐ **Fox Terrier**

NAME: _____ DATE: _____

NOTES: _____

_____

☐ **French Bulldog**

NAME: _____ DATE: _____

NOTES: _____

_____

☐ **German Pinscher**

NAME: _____ DATE: _____

NOTES: _____

_____

☐ **German Shepherd Dog**

NAME: _____ DATE: _____

NOTES: _____

_____

☐ German Wirehaired Pointer

NAME: _____ DATE: _____

NOTES: _____

_____

☐ Giant Schnauzer

NAME: _____ DATE: _____

NOTES: _____

_____

☐ Golden Retriever

NAME: _____ DATE: _____

NOTES: _____

_____

☐ Gordon Setter

NAME: _____ DATE: _____

NOTES: _____

_____

☐ Great Dane

NAME: _____ DATE: _____

NOTES: _____

_____

☐ Great Pyrenees

NAME: _____ DATE: _____

NOTES: _____

_____

☐ Greater Swiss Mountain Dog

NAME: _____ DATE: _____

NOTES: _____

_____

☐ Greyhound

NAME: _____ DATE: _____

NOTES: _____

_____

☐ Havanese

NAME: _____ DATE: _____

NOTES: _____

_____

☐ Ibizan Hound

NAME: _____ DATE: _____

NOTES: _____

_____

☐ Icelandic Sheepdog

NAME: _____ DATE: _____

NOTES: _____

_____

☐ Irish Setter

NAME: _____ DATE: _____

NOTES: _____

_____

☐ Irish Terrier

NAME: _____ DATE: _____

NOTES: _____

_____

☐ Irish Wolfhound

NAME: _____ DATE: _____

NOTES: _____

_____

☐ Jack Russell Terrier

NAME: _____ DATE: _____

NOTES: _____

_____

☐ Japanese Chin

NAME: _____ DATE: _____

NOTES: _____

_____

☐ Keeshond

NAME: _____ DATE: _____

NOTES: _____

_____

☐ Kerry Blue Terrier

NAME: _____ DATE: _____

NOTES: _____

_____

☐ Kuvasz

NAME: _____ DATE: _____

NOTES: _____

_____

☐ Labrador Retriever

NAME: _____ DATE: _____

NOTES: _____

_____

☐ Lakeland Terrier

NAME: _____ DATE: _____

NOTES: _____

_____

☐ Lhasa Apso

NAME: _____ DATE: _____

NOTES: _____

_____

☐ Löwchen

NAME: _____ DATE: _____

NOTES: _____

_____

☐ Maltese

NAME: _____ DATE: _____

NOTES: _____

_____

☐ Manchester Terrier

NAME: _____ DATE: _____

NOTES: _____

_____

☐ Mastiff

NAME: _____ DATE: _____

NOTES: _____

_____

☐ Neapolitan Mastiff

NAME: _____ DATE: _____

NOTES: _____

_____

☐ Newfoundland

NAME: _____ DATE: _____

NOTES: _____

_____

☐ Norfolk Terrier

NAME: _____ DATE: _____

NOTES: _____

_____

☐ Norwegian Elkhound

NAME: _____ DATE: _____

NOTES: _____

_____

☐ Norwich Terrier

NAME: _____ DATE: _____

NOTES: _____

_____

☐ Nova Scotia Duck Tolling Retriever

NAME: _____ DATE: _____

NOTES: _____

_____

☐ Old English Sheepdog

NAME: _____ DATE: _____

NOTES: _____

_____

☐ Otterhound

NAME: _____ DATE: _____

NOTES: _____

_____

☐ Papillon

NAME: _____ DATE: _____

NOTES: _____

_____

☐ Pekingese

NAME: _____ DATE: _____

NOTES: _____

_____

☐ Pembroke Welsh Corgi

NAME: _____ DATE: _____

NOTES: _____

_____

☐ Pharaoh Hound

NAME: _____ DATE: _____

NOTES: _____

_____

☐ Plott Hound

NAME: _____ DATE: _____

NOTES: _____

_____

☐ Pointer

NAME: _____ DATE: _____

NOTES: _____

_____

☐ Pomeranian

NAME: _____ DATE: _____

NOTES: _____

_____

☐ Poodle

NAME: _____ DATE: _____

NOTES: _____

_____

☐ **Portuguese Water Dog**

NAME: _____ DATE: _____

NOTES: _____

_____

☐ **Pug**

NAME: _____ DATE: _____

NOTES: _____

_____

☐ **Puli**

NAME: _____ DATE: _____

NOTES: _____

_____

☐ **Pumi**

NAME: _____ DATE: _____

NOTES: _____

_____

☐ **Rat Terrier**

NAME: _____ DATE: _____

NOTES: _____

_____

☐ **Rhodesian Ridgeback**

NAME: _____ DATE: _____

NOTES: _____

_____

☐ **Rottweiler**

NAME: _____ DATE: _____

NOTES: _____

_____

☐ **Saint Bernard**

NAME: _____ DATE: _____

NOTES: _____

_____

☐ **Saluki**

NAME: _____ DATE: _____

NOTES: _____

_____

☐ **Samoyed**

NAME: _____ DATE: _____

NOTES: _____

_____

☐ **Schnauzer**

NAME: _____ DATE: _____

NOTES: _____

_____

☐ **Scottish Deerhound**

NAME: _____ DATE: _____

NOTES: _____

_____

☐ **Scottish Terrier**

NAME: _____ DATE: _____

NOTES: _____

_____

☐ **Sealyham Terrier**

NAME: _____ DATE: _____

NOTES: _____

_____

☐ **Shetland Sheepdog**

NAME: _____ DATE: _____

NOTES: _____

_____

☐ **Shiba Inu**

NAME: _____ DATE: _____

NOTES: _____

_____

☐ **Shih Tzu**

NAME: _____ DATE: _____

NOTES: _____

_____

☐ **Siberian Husky**

NAME: _____ DATE: _____

NOTES: _____

_____

☐ **Silky Terrier**

NAME: _____ DATE: _____

NOTES: _____

_____

☐ **Skye Terrier**

NAME: _____ DATE: _____

NOTES: _____

_____

☐ **Soft-Coated Wheaten Terrier**

NAME: _____ DATE: _____

NOTES: _____

_____

☐ **Spanish Water Dog**

NAME: _____ DATE: _____

NOTES: _____

_____

☐ **Staffordshire Bull Terrier**

NAME: _____ DATE: _____

NOTES: _____

_____

☐ **Sussex Spaniel**

NAME: _____ DATE: _____

NOTES: _____

_____

☐ Tibetan Mastiff

NAME: _____ DATE: _____

NOTES: _____

_____

☐ Tibetan Terrier

NAME: _____ DATE: _____

NOTES: _____

_____

☐ Vizsla

NAME: _____ DATE: _____

NOTES: _____

_____

☐ Weimaraner

NAME: _____ DATE: _____

NOTES: _____

_____

☐ Welsh Springer Spaniel

NAME: _____ DATE: _____

NOTES: _____

_____

☐ Welsh Terrier

NAME: _____ DATE: _____

NOTES: _____

_____

☐ West Highland White Terrier

NAME: _____ DATE: _____

NOTES: _____

_____

☐ Whippet

NAME: _____ DATE: _____

NOTES: _____

_____

☐ Wirehaired Pointing Griffon

NAME: _____ DATE: _____

NOTES: _____

_____

☐ Xoloitzcuintli

NAME: _____ DATE: _____

NOTES: _____

_____

☐ Yorkshire Terrier

NAME: _____ DATE: _____

NOTES: _____

_____

Mixed Breeds

Of course, not all dogs are just one breed! There are lots of amazing mixed-breed dogs out there, and you may not even know what kind of dog you're meeting. Read on for some examples of common mixes and ways to track dogs who have even more interesting qualities than their breed.

- **Cavachon:** Cavalier King Charles Spaniel and Bichon Frise mix

- **Cavapoo:** Cavalier King Charles Spaniel and Poodle mix

- **Chiweenie:** Chihuahua and Dachshund mix

- **Cockapoo:** Cocker Spaniel and Poodle mix

- **Corgidor:** Corgi and Labrador Retriever mix

- **Goldendoodle:** Golden Retriever and Poodle mix

- **Labradoodle:** Labrador Retriever and Poodle mix

- **Pomsky:** Pomeranian and Siberian Husky mix

- **Puggle:** Pug and Beagle mix

- **Yorkipoo:** Yorkshire Terrier and Poodle mix

More Dogs to Look For!

Shaggy dog

NAME: _____ DATE: _____

NOTES: _____

_____

Spotted dog

NAME: _____ DATE: _____

NOTES: _____

_____

Large dog

NAME: _____ DATE: _____

NOTES: _____

_____

Tiny dog

NAME: _____ DATE: _____

NOTES: _____

_____

Brindle dog (brindle means a shade of brown mixed with another color. Some people say it looks like tiger stripes!)

NAME: _____ DATE: _____

NOTES: _____

_____

Dog in a sweater

NAME: _____ DATE: _____

NOTES: _____

_____

Service dog (Just look! Don't pet!)

NAME: _____ DATE: _____

NOTES: _____

_____

Dog who has a human name

NAME: _____ DATE: _____

NOTES: _____

_____

Dog who is named after someone famous

NAME: _____ DATE: _____

NOTES: _____

_____

Dog in a stroller

NAME: _____ DATE: _____

NOTES: _____

_____

Dog with curly hair

NAME: _____ DATE: _____

NOTES: _____

_____

Dog with different-colored eyes

NAME: _____ DATE: _____

NOTES: _____

_____

Dog who has your own name

NAME: _____ DATE: _____

NOTES: _____

_____

Dog who doesn't want you to stop petting him

NAME: _____ DATE: _____

NOTES: _____

_____

Dog in a costume

NAME: _____ DATE: _____

NOTES: _____

_____

Puppy

NAME: _____ DATE: _____

NOTES: _____

_____

Senior dog

NAME: _____ DATE: _____

NOTES: _____

_____

More Fun Facts about Dogs!

- **Chow Chows** and **Shar Peis** both have blue tongues!

- Dogs who are all white, or who have a piebald (patches of two different colors, most often black and white) or merle pattern (patches of different colors in a solid-colored coat) coat are more likely than other dogs to be deaf. The genes that create these fur patterns are related to a lack of cells that make pigment in blood vessels. This damages the cochlea, a part of the inner ear necessary for hearing.

- **Samoyeds** smile so they won't drool. The shape of their mouth stops drool from dripping down. Samoyeds are originally from Siberia, where the climate is extremely cold. If they drooled in such conditions, the drool would freeze on their face!

- **Basenjis** don't bark. Instead, they make a noise that sounds like a yodel.

- The **Norwegian Lundehund** has six toes on each paw.

- **Dalmatians** are born white, without any spots. Their spots appear when they are about 4 weeks old.

- A **Basset Hound**'s long, floppy ears are more than just cute. They also help lift smells to their nose. The loose skin under their chin and next to their ears is called a *dewlap*. It helps trap odors so the Basset can follow a scent. The Bloodhound is the only kind of dog who has a better sense of smell than a Basset Hound.

- **Australian Shepherds**, **Australian Cattle Dogs** (aka Blue Heelers), **Dalmatians**, and **Huskies** are more likely than other breeds to have two different-colored eyes.

- A **Shar-Pei**'s floppy skin folds are designed to protect him from attack. The floppy skin makes it hard to grab hold of a Shar-Pei or cause damage to his body. Shar-Peis were originally bred to protect livestock or hunt.

- Any color **Labrador** (black, chocolate, and yellow) can have any and all color puppies in a single litter. Separate genes determine coat color in this breed. Only when two yellow Labs mate do they have yellow puppies.

Conclusion
All Dogs Are Good Dogs

Some people collect stamps, video games, or books. I collect stories of dogs to show the world that each dog is amazing in their own way. Some dogs' stories are courageous, some are sad, some are happy, and some are funny. Their stories bring people together as we see a bit of ourselves, our families, or our own dog in them.

Dogs are wonderful pets. They celebrate with you on good days and cheer you up on bad days. But even more important, dogs are our helpers, our best friends, and our family members. The next time you see a dog, I hope you can pet that dog and make a new dog and human friend.

Acknowledgments

Thank you to Taylor Veterinary Hospital and Dr. Chad Smith. We appreciate how well you have taken care of our animals over the years, and we thank you for helping with this book.

Thank you to Retrieving Freedom. We are grateful you took the time to teach us about service dogs. Thank you for helping with this book.

Thank you to Melissa Edwards and Alex Arnold for making this book a reality. We could not have done it without your encouragement and advice.

Thank you to all the wonderful dogs and their caregivers who have allowed Gideon to tell their story and share their pictures. We are grateful for your kindness.

More about Dogs!

Books

. . . .

A Dog Called Homeless by Sarah Lean
   (Katherine Tegan Books, 2014)

Because of Winn-Dixie by Kate DiCamillo
   (Candlewick Press, 2020)

*Dog Training for Kids: Fun and Easy Ways to Care for
   Your Furry Friend* by Vanessa Estrada Marin
   (Z Kids Books, 2019)

How to Steal a Dog by Barbara O'Connor
   (Farrar, Straus & Giroux, 2009)

Love That Dog by Sharon Creech
   (HarperCollins, 2001)

Rescue and Jessica: A Life-Changing Friendship
   by Jessica Kensky and Patrick Downes
   (Candlewick Press, 2018)

Saving Winslow by Sharon Creech
   (HarperCollins, 2018)

Shiloh by Phyllis Reynolds Naylor
(Atheneum, 2012)

The Dog Encyclopedia for Kids by Tammy Gagne
(Capstone, 2017)

Wish by Barbara O'Connor
(Farrar, Straus & Giroux, 2016)

Movies
. . . .

Bolt (2008)

Homeward Bound (1993)

Lassie (1994)

101 Dalmatians (1996)

The Secret Life of Pets (2016)

Online Sources

For a full list of sources consulted in the writing of this book, visit quirkbooks.com/petthatdog.

The **AMERICAN KENNEL CLUB** website provides a wealth of information on dog breeds, behaviors, and personalities. Visit AKC.org to search for a specific topic, especially training tips (crate, clicker, potty, leash) and helpful facts like these:

Bovsun, Mara. "How to Potty Train Puppies: A Comprehensive Guide for Success." Mar. 2, 2019. www.akc.org/expert-advice/training/how-to-potty-train-a-puppy.

Gibeault, Stephanie. "How to Read Dog Body Language." Jan. 27, 2020. www.akc.org/expert-advice/training/how-to-read-dog-body-language.

Gibeault, Stephanie. "Why Does My Dog Sniff Everything?" Nov. 7, 2019. www.akc.org/expert-advice/training/why-does-my-dog-sniff-everything.

Rakosky, Erin. "What You Should Know About Canine Deafness." American Kennel Club, Sept. 15, 2016.

www.akc.org/expert-advice/health/what-you-should-know-about-canine-deafness.

Sharpe, Shannon. "How to Crate Train Your Dog in 9 Easy Steps." Dec. 23, 2019. www.akc.org/expert-advice/training/how-to-crate-train-your-dog-in-9-easy-steps.

"Which Dogs Are Hypoallergenic? These Breeds Come Close." American Kennel Club, July 31, 2019. www.akc.org/expert-advice/lifestyle/hypoallergenic-dog-breeds/.

"Why Do Chow Chows Have Blue Tongues?" Apr. 24, 2019, www.akc.org/expert-advice/lifestyle/why-do-chow-chows-have-blue-tongues.

"Why Do Small Dogs Live Longer?" Mar. 23, 2015. www.akc.org/expert-advice/health/why-do-small-dogs-live-longer.